Harry Houdini
A Magical Life

written by Elizabeth MacLeod

Kids Can Press

To John Venner, with best wishes for a magical life

Consultant: David Ben, magic consultant

Sources: In researching this book I found the following books helpful: *Spellbinder: The Life of Harry Houdini* by Tom Lalicki and *Houdini!!!* by Kenneth Silverman.

Acknowledgments: Special thanks to David Ben for reviewing my manuscript and sharing his incredible knowledge about magic and Harry. I so appreciate the time he took to read the book and answer my questions.

Chris McClymont is a terrific editor and friend. Many thanks for the care she put into this book and for the fun meetings. Thanks also to series editor Valerie Wyatt for her help.

It is always wonderful to work with designer Karen Powers and I'm grateful to her for her incredibly creative solutions. I'm always amazed by Patricia Buckley's diligence and imagination in suggesting and obtaining photos. I'm very lucky to have such a terrific team working on this series of books.

Thanks also to the entire Kids Can Press team, especially Sheila Barry, Karen Boersma, Valerie Hussey and everyone in the Technical Services Department.

Many thanks to Dad, John and Douglas for their continuing support. And very special thanks and love to Paul, who brings real magic into my life.

Kids Can Press acknowledges the financial support of the Government of Ontario, through the Ontario Media Development Corporation's Ontario Book Initiative; the Ontario Arts Council; the Canada Council for the Arts; and the Government of Canada, through the BPIDP, for our publishing activity.

Published in Canada by
Kids Can Press Ltd.
29 Birch Avenue
Toronto, ON M4V 1E2

Published in the U.S. by
Kids Can Press Ltd.
2250 Military Road
Tonawanda, NY 14150

www.kidscanpress.com

Series editor: Valerie Wyatt
Edited by Christine McClymont
Designed by Karen Powers
Printed and bound in China

The hardcover edition of this book is smyth sewn casebound.
The paperback edition of this book is limp sewn with a drawn-on cover.

CM 05 0 9 8 7 6 5 4 3 2 1
CM PA 05 0 9 8 7 6 5 4 3 2 1

National Library of Canada Cataloguing in Publication Data

MacLeod, Elizabeth
    Harry Houdini : a magical life / written by Elizabeth MacLeod.

Includes index.

ISBN 1-55337-769-9 (bound).   ISBN 1-55337-770-2 (pbk.)

1. Houdini, Harry, 1874–1926 — Juvenile literature. 2. Magicians — United States — Biography — Juvenile literature. 3. Escape artists — United States — Biography — Juvenile literature. I. Title.

GV1545.H8M33 2005   j793.8'092   C2004-906026-0

Photo credits

Every reasonable effort has been made to trace ownership of, and give accurate credit to, copyrighted material. Information that would enable the publisher to correct any discrepancies in future editions would be appreciated.

Abbreviations
t = top; b = bottom; c = center; l = left; r = right

Bettmann/Corbis/Magma: 9 (tr), 11 (l); **Chicago Historical Society/ICH-22859:** (cl); **Library of Congress:** 1, 3 (all), 4 (l), 5 (cl, tl, br), 6, 7 (cl, tr, cr, br), 8, 9 (bl, br), 10, 11 (tr, cr), 12, 13 (tl, tr, br), 14, 15 (all), 16, 17 (bl, tl, r), 19 (tr), 20 (all), 21 (all), 22, 23 (b, tr, cr), 25 (all), 27 (bl, tl, tr, br), 28 (b), 29 (all); **National Oceanic and Atmospheric Administration:** 17 (cl); **Outagamie Historical Society/Appleton, WI:** 4 (r), 18, 19 (b), 23 (tl), 26, 28 (t); **Harry Ransom Humanities Center/ The University of Texas at Austin/Performing Arts Collection:** 19 (l); **State Library of Victoria, Australia, H88.50/5:** 7 (bl); **The Museum of the City of New York:** 19 (cr); **The Museum of the City of New York/ Bandit's Roost by Jacob A. Riis/ The Jacob A. Riis Collection:** 9 (tl).

Kids Can Press is a **corus**™ Entertainment company

Contents

Meet Harry Houdini

"Never try to fool children. They expect nothing and therefore see everything."
— Harry

One of Harry's most amazing stunts was the Milk Can Escape. He was handcuffed, chained and squished into a milk can full of water. Then he had to escape from this solid metal container before he drowned.

Have you ever been dazzled by a magic show? Most magicians get started on their careers after watching a magician perform. That's how the most famous magician ever, Harry Houdini, got hooked on magic.

Walking Through a Brick Wall, Water-Torture Cell Escape, Needle Swallowing — these are just a few of the magic tricks and escapes Harry performed to amaze audiences around the world. Some of his tricks were so difficult and dangerous that few of today's best-trained magicians dare attempt them.

Behind Harry's magic was a lot of hard work and training. He wasn't a big man, but he exercised and became very strong. He was always practicing and thinking of new escapes and tricks. Although Harry didn't have much education, he taught himself everything he needed to know to excel as a magician.

Harry thought he was a great magician and wasn't afraid to say so. He also loved a good story and sometimes even made up things so he'd sound more amazing. Harry's stories were so convincing that it can be difficult to know the truth about his life.

Read on to find out what *is* known about Harry's life. How did he become the world's best-known magician? Could he actually escape from handcuffs? Was he able to make an elephant disappear? What was Harry really like?

Harry Houdini

Harry was born Ehrich Weisz (later spelled Weiss), but he changed his name to Harry Houdini when he began performing.

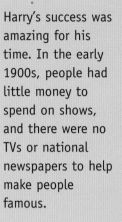

There weren't many who knew the secrets behind my tricks. My wife, Bess, was one of the few people I trusted.

Harry's success was amazing for his time. In the early 1900s, people had little money to spend on shows, and there were no TVs or national newspapers to help make people famous.

Standing less than 168 cm (5 ft., 6 in.) tall, Harry had blazing blue eyes and thick, curly black hair.

EUROPE'S ECLIPSING SENSATION
HOUDINI
THE WORLD'S HANDCUFF KING & PRISON BREAKER

"NOTHING CAN HO HOUDI A PRISO

What an incredible performer and showman! Harry could create a sense of wonder around his tricks that dazzled audiences.

HOW DOES HOUDINI DO WHAT HOUDINI DOES?

HOUDINI---The name conjures up Jails, Prisons, Handcuffs, Bolts, and Bars, for he is the creator of that branch of work. A daring man, skillful, careful entertainer, and never having met with defeat, he is open to accept any challenge during his engagement at the Orpheum Theatre the coming week, that will interest the general public. When not accepting a challenge, during his regulation performance, he will introduce his original invention, "The Chinese Water Torture Cell." Houdini is the only legitimate jailbreaker in the world and was proclaimed by Theodore Roosevelt "The Most Stupendous Mystifier I Have Ever Seen." Let us hope he will receive some interesting challenges, and that our local carpenters, locksmiths and other craftsmen will construct something from which Houdini cannot extricate himself.

The Genius of Escape
HOUDINI
Who Will Startle and Amaze

MAIN 4161
Orpheum
Orpheum Circuit Vaudeville
ONE WEEK ONLY
Starting Saturday Matinee

MAY 5th
SAME POPULAR PRICES—NEVER CHANGE
Daily Matinees, 15c to 50c   Every Night, 15c to $1.00

One of Harry's acts was escaping from heavy chains, tires and locks. He could do it in just 19 minutes.

Little Ehrich

"October 28, 1883, was the date of my first appearance before an audience. I appeared as a contortionist and trapeze performer ..."
— Harry

1877
3½ YEARS OF AGE

Here are Ehrich and his little brother Theo before they left Budapest. Ehrich later helped Theo become the magician known as "Hardeen."

Harry made up many stories about his life, especially about his childhood. For instance, he claimed he was born in the United States, though records prove he was born in Budapest, Hungary, in 1874. Maybe Harry thought his American audiences would like him more if they thought that he was American, too.

Ehrich Weisz was Harry's real name, but the family's last name was later changed to Weiss. His father, Mayer Samuel Weiss, worked as a rabbi (a leader of a Jewish congregation). When he couldn't get a job in Budapest, he left the family, sailed to the United States and became the rabbi of a congregation in Appleton, Wisconsin. Ehrich was only two at the time. Two years later, in 1878, Ehrich's father had saved enough money to bring his family to join him.

Ehrich's mother, Cecilia, had never seen a baby like him. He rarely cried and slept very little. He always seemed to be awake and staring. But Cecilia had other things to think about. She had seven children to look after and her husband's salary was small. It soon became smaller. In 1882, Ehrich's father's congregation in Appleton let him go. So the family moved to nearby Milwaukee, Wisconsin's largest city.

It was in Milwaukee that Ehrich saw his first magic show. His father took him to see Dr. Lynn, a magician whose gruesome act included a dismembering trick. He'd slash off the arms, legs and head of a man, then magically reassemble him. Ehrich was astounded.

In Milwaukee, the family moved five times, to smaller and smaller homes. There were no laws to make kids attend school, so Ehrich took whatever jobs he could to support his family. He once made money by standing motionless on a wintry sidewalk holding out his cap. As snow piled up, so did the coins in his hat. Ehrich hid the money in his clothes, headed home, then told his mother to shake him. Like magic, coins flew out! Ehrich was already performing, as he would for the rest of his life.

With his father working only occasionally, there was never enough money, despite Ehrich's efforts. How would the family survive?

Appleton

Milwaukee

WISCONSIN

IOWA

ILLINOIS

INDIANA

MONTANA

Ehrich's mother, Cecilia Steiner Weiss, had a stepson (Herman) and two children (Nathan and William) who were older than Ehrich, and three (Theodore, Leopold and Carrie Gladys) who were younger.

AUSTRIA

SLOVENIA

HUNGARY

Budapest

CROATIA

ITALY

What a life! I was just four years old when I crossed the Atlantic Ocean for the first time.

Born in Budapest, Hungary, Ehrich was four when his family came to the United States. They moved to Appleton, Wisconsin, and four years later to Milwaukee.

Neither Ehrich's father, Rabbi Weiss, nor his mother fit in well in the United States. They never learned to speak English.

FOREPAUGH & SELLS BROTHERS
SHOWS COMBINED

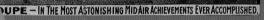
UPE – IN THE MOST ASTONISHING MID-AIR ACHIEVEMENTS EVER ACCOMPLISHED.

Trapeze artists amazed Ehrich. At age nine, he was an agile acrobat, performing in his neighborhood and making money his family badly needed. He called himself "Ehrich, the Prince of the Air."

Dr. Lynn, the magician, inspired eight-year-old Ehrich. In Dr. Lynn's show, he seemed to cut people up and put them back together again!

By the time Ehrich was eight, he was earning money by selling newspapers, running errands, shining shoes and more.

Runaway!

"We lived there, I mean starved there, several years. The less said on the subject the better."
— Harry

One of Ehrie's jobs in New York was errand boy. He also helped make metal tools and may have worked for a printer.

As he grew older, Ehrich found his family's poverty harder to bear. There was never enough money for food or heat. He did his best to earn money for his family, but there weren't many jobs a young boy could do. Maybe, thought Ehrich, there was work for him somewhere else. So, at age 12, he ran away from home.

Ehrich had planned to go to Galveston, Texas, but by mistake he jumped on the wrong train and landed in Kansas City, Missouri. He eventually ended up in Delavan, Wisconsin, just 80 km (50 mi.) from Milwaukee.

Ehrich never found work, but a kindly couple took him in and fed and cared for him for the summer. Meanwhile, Ehrich's dad had given up trying to find work in Milwaukee. He thought he might have a better chance in a bigger city. In 1887, he went to New York, and Ehrich joined him there, followed shortly by the whole family.

Ehrie, as Ehrich liked to be called now, heard about a job cutting fabric for neckties. But when he arrived to apply for the position, there was already a long line of people ahead of him. Ehrie's family was depending on him to get this job. What could he do?

Boldly marching to the front of the line, Ehrie grabbed the job sign and told the crowd that the position was filled. Then he went into the building, applied for the job and got it. Or is that what really happened? No one knows for sure — but that's what Ehrie told people because it made a good story.

Cutting neckties was a miserable, dirty job. But at work, Ehrie made a friend named Jacob Hyman. Determined to find better jobs and fascinated by magic, the teenagers decided to create a magic act. But first they needed a good name.

One of Ehrie's favorite magicians was a famous French showman called Jean-Eugène Robert-Houdin. Ehrie had heard that magicians sometimes added an "i" to the end of another magician's name to suggest they were like that person. So, at age 17, he created the last name "Houdini" for himself. The name "Harry" came from his nickname, Ehrie. Soon Harry and Jacob were performing magic tricks as "The Brothers Houdini."

Ehrie and his family lived in rundown apartment buildings in New York City. When Ehrie became successful, he rarely spoke about the poverty he'd experienced.

The name Houdini came from Jean-Eugène Robert-Houdin. This French magician used the latest technology and was one of the first magicians to perform in theaters rather than on street corners.

Despite working hard, Ehrie found time for swimming, boxing and running. Some of the racing medals here are real but others are fakes that Ehrie added for the photo.

Ehrie's spelling was often wrong (see how he spells Galveston) and his handwriting was always hard to read.

Even though I ran away, I made sure I wrote home.

A new act

"Our act is the supreme cabinet mystery in the World. [It] has been featured at … the Oxford London and has created a sensation in Europe, Australia, and America." — Harry

(This was one of Harry's stories. He and Bess hadn't yet performed in Europe or Australia.)

When Harry first met Bess Rahner, she was singing and dancing in an act called "The Floral Sisters."

Harry and Jacob left necktie cutting in 1891 to focus full-time on magic. Before Harry's father died in 1892, he made Harry promise to look after his mother. Harry loved her deeply, and no matter how little money he made, he always gave her some.

In 1893, the stock market fell, companies went bankrupt and thousands of people lost their jobs. People could barely afford food, let alone tickets for magic shows. Harry might have been tempted to go back to cutting neckties, but he stuck with his Brothers Houdini magic show.

The Brothers Houdini performed at the World's Fair in Chicago, but few people saw them. Their act was just one of a long line of shows and had to compete with many other attractions, including a huge Ferris wheel. Harry and Jacob also toured upstate New York and the American Midwest, performing in small theaters and with groups of low-paid performers including puppeteers, fire-eaters and giants.

One of Harry's most successful illusions or tricks was Needle Swallowing. He seemed to chew and swallow dozens of needles and a long piece of thread, then regurgitate the thread with the needles threaded on it. This illusion, which did not involve actually swallowing needles, amazed audiences throughout Harry's career. You can see Harry performing it on page 23.

Early in 1894, Jacob decided he wanted to perform on his own, so Jacob's brother Joe Hyman joined Harry. Then Joe was replaced by Harry's brother Theodore. But that spring, Harry met Bess Rahner, a singer and dancer. Three weeks later they were married. Bess became Harry's stage partner and the couple called themselves "The Houdinis."

Harry and Bess became famous for their illusion called Metamorphosis (it means transformation). It began with Harry stepping into a flannel bag, which was sealed shut. The bag was locked in a trunk, then the trunk was tied with thick ropes and wheeled into a curtained cabinet.

Standing at the open curtain, Bess announced, "Now then, I shall clap my hands three times, and at the third and last time I ask you to watch CLOSELY for — the — EFFECT!" Bess jerked the curtain closed and vanished, but instantly the curtain was reopened — by Harry! Bess was sealed in the bag in the still roped and padlocked trunk! Audiences applauded wildly. Was this the beginning of success for Harry?

Bess was Harry's best partner for Metamorphosis, the "cabinet mystery," because she was small, quick and willing to work hard.

In Harry's Color-Changing Handkerchief trick, a hankie switched color when he passed it through a seemingly empty tube.

THE HOUDINIS

PRESENT THEIR   MARVELLOUS MYSTERY

METAMORPHO

EXCHANGE MADE IN 3 SECONDS

The Greatest Novelty Mystery Act in th

The Brothers Houdini performed card tricks, pulled handkerchiefs out of candle flames and more.

My brother Theo and I appeared as The Brothers Houdini, but I was always the boss.

Tough times

"… any one in possession of my secret could laugh at locks just as heartily as I do."
— Harry

Contortionists (acrobats who can twist their bodies into almost impossible positions) fascinated Harry. He had to be a bit of a contortionist to escape from a straitjacket.

Harry and Bess dazzled audiences with Metamorphosis. But the crowd grew bored when Harry presented tricks that many other magicians could perform. Some people thought Harry spoke poorly with bad grammar and looked shabby in his old clothes. Harry knew to make it big he'd have to improve his act and present 20 minutes of mind-boggling magic.

In November 1895, Harry had the idea of being handcuffed before stepping into the Metamorphosis bag. When he emerged, the cuffs hung open from his wrists. But audiences weren't impressed — they assumed he'd used trick handcuffs. So Harry began showing up at police stations and unlocking their cuffs. Soon newspapers were running articles about his stunts and giving him the publicity he craved.

The Houdinis toured with various groups across North America, performing magic, comedy, music — anything that paid. While in eastern Canada, Harry visited a mental hospital and watched violent patients try to break free from their straitjackets (long-sleeved jackets that bound the patients' arms).

Of course, Harry had to try escaping from one. It took seven tries and left him bruised and bloody, but he managed to wriggle out. Straitjacket escapes would later become an important part of his act.

In 1898, Harry added a new kind of act — performing séances on stage. He made ghostly hands and faces appear and pretended to pass on messages from dead people to their grieving families. But Harry felt bad hoaxing people and taking advantage of their sorrow.

Despite some success, there were times when Harry and Bess had nothing to eat. At the end of the year, they were back in New York, out of work and living with Harry's mother. Ready to give up, Harry ran an ad in a newspaper offering to sell all of his magic tricks and secrets for $20. There were no buyers.

While Harry was deciding whether to quit magic, he had to perform a few shows that he'd promised to give. In early 1899, big-time theater manager Martin Beck caught Harry's act in St. Paul, Minnesota.

Beck gave Harry his big break. The manager agreed to book Harry and Bess into top theaters, but suggested they concentrate on escapes. Soon Harry was in demand at the best vaudeville houses, performing in variety shows along with singers, contortionists, dancing dogs and jugglers.

Harry presented card tricks using the nickname "King of Cards" or "Cardo." He also performed as the "Great Wizard," "Professor Murat" and "Projea the Wild Man." None of these acts succeeded.

At first, people thought I used trick handcuffs for my escapes. When I used police cuffs and still escaped, audiences were amazed by me.

There wasn't a pair of handcuffs Harry couldn't get out of — or so he claimed.

Harry and Bess toured with many groups, including the Welsh Brothers Circus.

IN THE CIRCUS. THE HOUDINIS ARE AT THE RIGHT OF THE FRONT ROW. MRS. HOUDINI WEARS A LORD FAUNTLEROY SUIT.

International star

Harry could now afford expensive suits for his show. But off stage, he was a sloppy dresser — he was always thinking about magic and escapes, not clothes.

Before he got into vaudeville, Harry had been paid just $25 a week, if he got paid at all. Now his salary quickly soared to $400 a week — about what most families lived on for a whole year! He could finally afford to wear elegant clothes to impress audiences.

But Harry wanted more spectators to dazzle. He also disliked working for someone else and having to pay Martin Beck a part of his salary. So Harry and Bess headed for Europe. They arrived in England with no shows lined up but lots of confidence — and high hopes that Harry's genius for publicity would open up new audiences to them.

Harry's amazing escape from the "Mirror Cuffs" on March 17, 1904, made him famous in England. These handcuffs got their name from the *London Daily Illustrated Mirror* newspaper. Staff with the paper found a special pair of "unpickable" handcuffs — which a blacksmith had taken five years to make — and challenged Harry to break out of them.

On stage, the Mirror Cuffs were snapped around Harry's wrists. Then Harry disappeared into his cabinet. In less than an hour, Harry appeared again. But the cuffs were still on — he was only asking to have them removed so he could take off his jacket. The newspaper's representative refused to do it — he was worried that Harry would learn how to escape from the cuffs if he watched them being unlocked.

So Harry, still handcuffed, wriggled a jackknife out of a pocket, opened the knife with his teeth and slashed at his jacket until it fell off. Then he headed back into the cabinet. In ten minutes he was out, with the cuffs hanging from his hands! It was an amazing show, especially because, for most of it, the spellbound audience was staring at a curtained cabinet.

Then Harry and Bess headed for Germany. Before Harry was allowed to perform there, his act had to be reviewed by the police. He was nervous because people were put in jail in Germany for trying to fool the public, and you might say that's what Harry planned to do. But the police approved his act, and audiences flocked to his shows.

In Paris, France, Harry hired seven bald-headed men for a publicity stunt. With one letter painted on top of each bald head, the men would sit in a row in sidewalk cafés wearing hats. Then they bowed their heads and took off their hats, one by one, until they spelled out "HOUDINI"!

By 1905, Harry was earning as much as $2150 a week. It was time for him and Bess to return to America and become big stars at home, too.

Harry performed in England, Scotland, Germany, France, Holland, Denmark and Russia.

"Most of my success in Europe was due to the fact that I lost no time in stirring up local interest in every town I played. The first thing was to break out of jail."
— Harry

Bess and I smuggled our little dog, Charlie, across country borders.

In Germany, Harry had many nicknames, including "Escape King," the "Unexplained Riddle" and "King of Handcuffs."

CIRCUS BUSCH
Houdini

Sometimes Bess still assisted Harry on stage. Harry said they were "two young (?) people, roaming around trying to make an honest million."

Back in the USA

"The easiest way to attract a crowd is to let it be known that at a given time and a given place some one is going to attempt something that in the event of failure will mean sudden death."
— Harry

Harry rarely slept more than five hours a night. "I have tried through many a sleepless night to invent schemes to make an audience appreciate some worthy effort of mine," he said.

Harry and Bess came home in the summer of 1905. Harry had missed his mother and was glad to be back in the United States. During a visit from Europe in 1904, he had bought a house in New York for $25 000. (Today it would cost more than $2 000 000.) He and Bess hoped to raise a family there, but they never had children.

Their New York house became both a home and a lab where, for instance, Harry practiced holding his breath underwater in a huge tub. To prepare for an escape he had in mind, Harry also practiced enduring cold water until he could stand temperatures barely above freezing.

By now Harry spoke well and looked very polished on stage. As he toured the United States, performing from Boston to San Francisco, he complimented his audiences and seemed delighted to perform for them. But he knew he had to develop more amazing stunts to hold their interest.

While in Rochester, New York, in 1907, Harry performed his first Manacled Bridge Jump. ("Manacled" is another word for "handcuffed.") The scene was the Weighlock Bridge. Thousands began gathering hours beforehand to see Harry, shackled in handcuffs and chains, jump into the water far below. Harry waited till the crowd was silent, then took a deep breath … and leaped off the bridge.

The onlookers held their breath. Would Harry free himself or would he drown? Fifteen seconds after Harry hit the water, a bare arm thrust up above the surface, holding the open cuffs. He'd done it!

How did Harry perform his amazing escapes? Few people know for sure, but many have tried to guess. Before attempting an escape, Harry would often select people from the audience to test the locks and make sure there was no trickery. Then he shook hands with them all. Maybe the last person to shake hands with Harry was a friend who passed him a lock-opening pick.

Sometimes, just before he was locked up, Bess gave Harry a kiss. Could she have passed a pick from her mouth to his? Harry performed his escapes almost naked, which meant he couldn't hide anything in his clothes. Men carefully searched Harry's mouth and nose — but there are other places where he could have concealed a pick, including the thick skin on the soles of his feet.

If there was any trickery involved, no one could spot it. That was Harry's special skill.

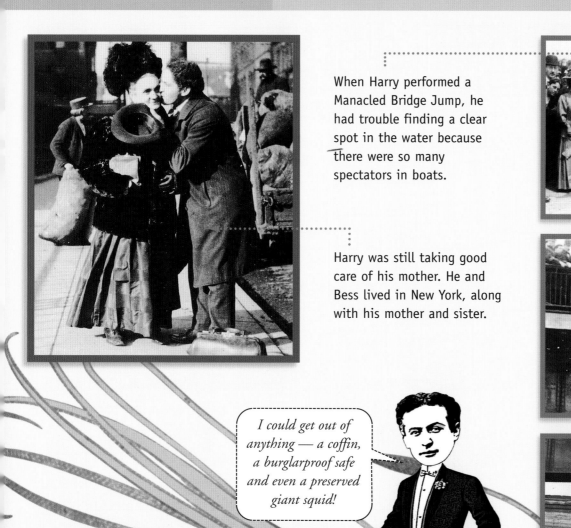

When Harry performed a Manacled Bridge Jump, he had trouble finding a clear spot in the water because there were so many spectators in boats.

Harry was still taking good care of his mother. He and Bess lived in New York, along with his mother and sister.

> *I could get out of anything — a coffin, a burglarproof safe and even a preserved giant squid!*

In 1906 Harry began producing the *Conjurers' Monthly Magazine*. Over the years he also filled his New York home with more than 5000 books and posters about magic. His collection is now at the Library of Congress.

Milk can magic

"Ladies and Gentlemen, my latest invention — the Milk Can. I will be placed in this can and it will be filled with water … I will attempt to escape." — Harry

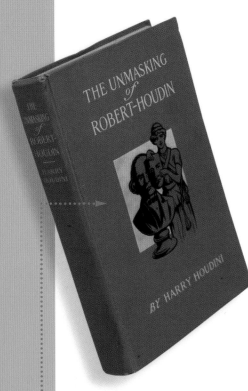

In 1908, Harry wrote *The Unmasking of Robert-Houdin*, which criticized the magician whose name he'd taken. Harry always wanted to be better than everyone else.

The Milk Can Escape was Harry's next famous escape. From the first time he performed it in 1908, it enchanted audiences.

Wearing just a bathing suit and handcuffs, Harry pointed to a large, old-fashioned milk can into which he was about to disappear and announced, "Should anything happen, and should I fail to appear within a certain time, my assistants will open the curtains, rush in, smash the Milk Can and do everything possible to save my life …"

Then Harry squeezed into the milk can, which was filled with water. The lid was locked down and a cabinet was slipped around the can. Harry had to escape from the inky darkness — or drown.

Harry's assistant stood by with an ax. Spectators tried to hold their breath for long as Harry held *his*. A band played as the seconds ticked by on a huge clock. After a minute, most people gave up and took a breath, but there was no sign of Harry. The audience became hysterical. After almost three grueling minutes, Harry breathlessly appeared.

Actually, Harry had escaped quickly from the milk can, but he waited to show himself just to get the audience more excited. How did Harry escape so fast? The collar of the can *seemed* to be tightly bolted in place by many heavy rivets. The can had been examined by members of the audience — but were the rivets real? Behind the cabinet, Harry kept his secrets to himself.

In 1908 and 1909, Harry and Bess were back in Europe, amazing audiences. While there, Harry became fascinated by airplanes. He'd always been intrigued by scientific breakthroughs and thought of himself as an inventor. While in Europe, he even bought his own biplane (a plane with two pairs of wings).

When Harry got a good offer to perform in Australia, he couldn't turn it down. During the many weeks it took to sail down under — planes couldn't fly very far then — he hoped to relax and recover from the strain of performing. Instead, Harry was seasick the whole way. But he was being paid for his travel time so he thought it was a great deal.

In January 1910, Harry, Bess and the biplane, also on the ship, arrived in Australia. Harry was determined to win the award for the first person to fly in Australia. Despite competition from rival pilots, blistering temperatures and engine troubles, on March 18, 1910, Harry soared into the sky and claimed the prize.

Harry's Milk Can Escape was advertised with the slogan, "Failure means a drowning death!"

See my name on the plane? I never missed a chance for publicity.

Harry performed terrifying escapes and flew airplanes but he rarely drove a car — it made him too nervous!

Harry always performed the Milk Can Escape successfully, but an imitator drowned trying it.

Much more magic

In 1914, Harry had his picture taken in a group that included former US President Theodore Roosevelt. Harry wanted people to think they were friends, so he airbrushed everyone else out of the photo below.

Despite suffering from seasickness, Harry spent the next three years crisscrossing the Atlantic Ocean, touring England, Europe and the United States. But he was forced to take a break in November 1911. During one of his escapes, he was strapped too tightly into a bag and received the first major injury of his long, daredevil career.

Harry ignored the pain for several weeks until he was forced to see a doctor. A ruptured blood vessel in one of his kidneys was the diagnosis. The doctor ordered Harry to rest for a few months and said if he kept performing such strenuous escapes, he'd be dead in a year. But Harry kept going, finishing the tour before he took a break. And, after only two weeks, he was back on stage. He just couldn't stop.

Always looking for sensational new acts, Harry combined two stunts to create the Underwater Box Escape. *Scientific American* magazine called it "one of the most remarkable tricks ever performed." On July 7, 1912, at New York Harbor, Harry was handcuffed and squeezed into a wooden crate. The box was dumped into the water, where it started to sink. But Harry quickly made his escape, leaving the box lid nailed shut and the cuffs inside.

Some people say Harry's next escape was his greatest ever. It was known as the Water-Torture Cell Escape, but Harry usually called it the "Upside Down" or "USD." This trick took more than three years to perfect before he began performing it in 1912.

In the USD, Harry dangled upside down in a slim glass case full of water, with heavy clamps holding his feet. In less than two minutes, Harry escaped, leaving the cuffs that had held his feet still locked. Audiences roared their approval.

July 1913 was supposed to be a great month for Harry. He legally changed his name to Harry Houdini, and he set sail for Europe, where he was to perform for the king of Sweden. But shortly after he started his show tour, he received a telegram that made him faint — his mother had died.

Harry and Bess caught the next ship back to New York. He insisted that his family not bury his mother immediately, as Jewish people usually do, but wait so that he could see her one last time. Harry got his wish, but he never got over his mother's death.

"I believe that [the Water-Torture Cell Escape] is the climax of all my studies and labors … Never will I be able to construct anything that will be more dangerous or difficult for me to do." — Harry

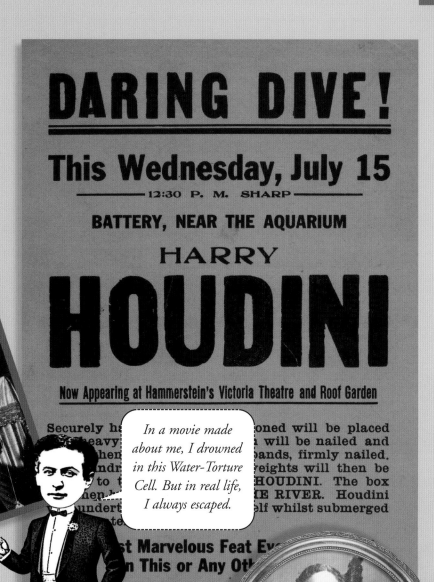

DARING DIVE!

This Wednesday, July 15
———— 12:30 P. M. SHARP ————

BATTERY, NEAR THE AQUARIUM

HARRY

HOUDINI

Now Appearing at Hammerstein's Victoria Theatre and Roof Garden

In a movie made about me, I drowned in this Water-Torture Cell. But in real life, I always escaped.

For the Underwater Box Escape, Harry was squished inside this thick pine box, which was tightly sealed with nails, heavy rope and metal bands.

Despite being married almost 20 years, Harry and Bess continued to leave love notes around their house for each other to find.

The disappearing elephant

"With due modesty, I recognize no one as my peer." — Harry

Harry bragged that making Jenny the elephant disappear was "the biggest vanish the world has ever seen."

After his visit to New Brunswick, in eastern Canada, years earlier, Harry had tried to entertain audiences by struggling out of a straitjacket. At that time, people weren't impressed — they figured the jacket was fake. But Harry never gave up on a good escape. In 1915 he found a way to perform the Suspended Straitjacket Escape and attract his biggest crowds ever.

This new version began outside, in front of a skyscraper. First Harry was tightly strapped into the straitjacket. His ankles were tied together and a long rope attached. Slowly Harry was hauled up by the rope until he dangled upside down many stories above the crowd below. As people watched, he writhed and jerked, at times squirming so hard that he was almost standing up. Within minutes, he wriggled out of the straitjacket and triumphantly let it fall to the ground.

The Suspended Straitjacket Escape put an incredible strain on Harry's whole body, especially his ankles. If he wasn't pulled up smoothly, he could smash against the building — he once cut his head badly on a window ledge. The trick was so dangerous it killed some other performers who attempted it.

In 1917, the United States joined World War I and Harry volunteered to fight. But he was considered too old, so he made his contribution to the war effort by giving free performances for soldiers, raising money and getting other magicians involved. He even gave away some of his secrets to teach soldiers useful things such as how to escape from handcuffs, untie ropes and survive underwater.

All his life, Harry performed without charge for many groups, including seniors, orphans and children in hospitals. He even developed a show for blind people in which he did mind-reading tricks.

In 1918 Harry performed at the Hippodrome, a gigantic theater in New York. He knew he needed a magic trick as enormous as the stage, so he decided to perform the Disappearing Elephant Trick. After members of the audience examined a huge wooden box, Harry led Jenny the elephant into it. The door on the box was closed and when Harry reopened it, Jenny was gone!

Actually, Jenny was still in the box, hidden behind a huge, tilted mirror. It made the box's sides look straight, though one was angled enough to conceal an elephant. The "vanish" got lots of publicity. Harry stayed at the Hippodrome for 19 weeks, the longest he'd ever performed in one place.

Harry first attempted the Suspended Straitjacket Escape in 1915. He performed it for the next three years in any city he visited that had skyscrapers.

In his Hippodrome show, Harry performed the Needle Swallowing Trick. Actually, he never swallowed the needles.

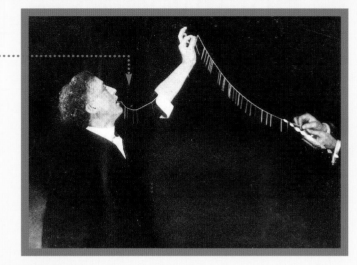

I always swallowed the needles "eye" first, so they could "see" where they were going. Get the joke?

How did Harry get out of a straitjacket? Among other things, he expanded his chest and held his shoulders wide while the jacket was being tightened around him. This gave him some room to move when he started squirming out of it.

This was Harry's view of the huge crowds below while he performed his Suspended Straitjacket Escape.

Hollywood star

"No illusion is good in a film, as we simply resort to camera trix, and the deed is did."
— Harry

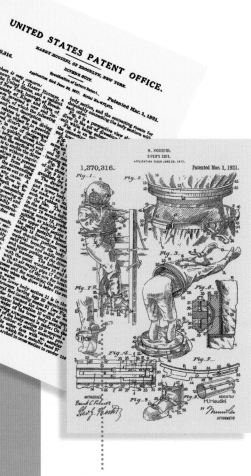

Harry was so interested in inventions and underwater escapes that he invented a diving suit.

The latest trends always caught Harry's interest. In the early 1900s he could see that movies were taking over from stage shows. In 1916 he started the Film Development Company to sell a fast, cheap process for developing movie film. Now he wanted to become a movie actor, too.

Harry's first movie was *The Master Mystery*, a 15-part series with a new adventure each week. This 1919 serial included impossible escapes and feats of great daring, such as Harry getting out of a collapsed cave and fighting a robot (probably one of the first robots ever seen in a movie). The film also featured a scene in which Harry showed how agile his toes were — he could use them almost like fingers. *The Master Mystery* became a major hit.

Later that year, Harry starred in *The Grim Game*. The climax showed Harry climbing from one biplane to another in mid-air, then surviving a terrifying crash. Harry had been willing to perform the stunt, but the director wouldn't risk it. A stuntman stood in for Harry in the plane, and the crash was accidental — luckily no one was hurt and it made for amazing action. However, Harry seemed to forget that a stand-in had actually done the stunt and began taking credit for it.

At the end of 1919, Harry sailed to Europe to perform the shows he'd had to postpone because of World War I. Audiences adored both his stage act and his movies, and he earned a fantastic $3750 or more each week.

Terror Island, Harry's third movie, was released in 1920. One year later he brought out *The Soul of Bronze*. In 1922 he starred in, wrote and produced *The Man from Beyond*. To make sure the film was a success, he added live magic performances to its showings. But each movie was less successful than the one before. Harry's sixth movie, *Haldane of the Secret Service*, was a flop and the last film he made.

It may have been a relief to Harry to get out of filmmaking. Movie audiences weren't impressed with his amazing stunts because they couldn't tell whether Harry was really performing them or just relying on camera trickery. As well, Harry broke bones and tore muscles while filming and was injured far more than he ever had been on stage.

You can still watch some of my great movies on video. Don't miss 'em!

Harry said this photo from *The Grim Game* was taken 1220 m (4000 ft.) up in the air. That made a good story, but the photo was actually shot on the ground.

Here's the French poster for Harry's film *The Master Mystery*. In France he was called "The Most Popular Man in the Entire World."

In the film *The Man from Beyond*, Harry played a man frozen in a wall of ice for 100 years before being thawed.

HOUDINI
LE MAÎTRE DU MYSTÈRE

GRAND ROMAN CINÉMA
Adapté par
M. J. PETITHUGUENIN

ÉDITÉ PAR
PATHÉ

PUBLIÉ DANS
L'ORDRE PUBLIC

E. G.

houdinize: to release or extricate oneself from (confinement, bonds, or the like), as by wriggling out.

By now Harry was so famous that he got a word based on his name into the 1920 edition of Funk & Wagnall's dictionary.

In *The Man from Beyond*, Harry wrestled on a cliff, escaped after being tied up in a wet sheet, and rescued his sweetheart at the top of Niagara Falls.

Séance scandals

"It takes a flimflammer to catch a flimflammer."
— Harry

Recognize me? I'm in disguise to expose a fake medium. My magnifying lenses give me a close look at any sneaky tricks.

Ever since his mother had died, Harry had been looking into spiritualism, the belief that dead people can communicate with the living. Many people were interested in spiritualism at that time, especially if they'd lost loved ones in World War I or during the deadly flu epidemic of 1918.

Harry was against mediums (people who claimed to be able to contact the dead) because he felt they took advantage of people's grief just to get their money. He also knew about their tricks, such as making spirit faces appear or objects mysteriously move, because he'd once done the same things himself (see page 12).

In England, Harry had become friends with Sir Arthur Conan Doyle, the famous author of the Sherlock Holmes books, and his wife. The couple both believed in spiritulism, and Lady Jean Doyle offered to contact Harry's mother. Harry was eager to hear from his mother, despite not really believing that this was possible.

Harry had a séance with Lady Doyle back in the United States. Page after page of greetings flowed from her pen, all supposedly from Cecilia. Harry didn't believe a word of it — mostly because the words were all in English, a language his mother barely knew.

Harry began to lecture against spiritualism. He exposed many mediums as frauds and made lots of enemies, but audiences loved Harry's explanations of the trickery. In one case, Harry said, a medium sewed his own pant cuffs to the carpet to prove that he wasn't moving about in the dark during a séance. When the lights were suddenly turned on, everyone was shocked to see him sneaking around in his underwear!

In 1924, Harry joined a group from *Scientific American* magazine to investigate psychics, including Boston's famous medium Mina Crandon, known as Margery. She said she could communicate with spirits through her dead brother and his "spirit bat." Margery also seemed to lift objects without touching them and to exude ectoplasm, a slime that supposedly shows the presence of a ghost. If Margery could prove she was the real thing, she'd win $2500 from *Scientific American*.

For months Harry's committee attended Margery's séances and argued about them. Finally all but one of the members agreed with Harry that Margery was a fraud. Margery was furious that she hadn't won the money. But she later said, "I respect Houdini more than any of the bunch. He has both feet on the ground all the time."

Here's Harry in the wooden box he put Margery into during séances. He wanted to see if the "spirits" could still move objects while Margery was in the box.

Harry set up this photo to show how a medium might fool people. In the dark, many would believe this person was a real spirit.

PALACE
B.F. KEITH THEATRE

MOST MAGNIFICENT PLAYHOUSE IN THE WORLD. CLEVELAND'S
GREATEST INSTITUTION OF AMUSEMENT
STARTING TODAY, TWICE DAILY, 2:15 AND 8:15

GO TODAY! Do Not Buy Seats From Speculators

2D BIG WEEK!
GREATEST SENSATION IN YEARS
**THE ACTUAL EXPOSE
OF A WORLD PROBLEM**
METHODS OF FAKE MEDIUMS
BROUGHT BEFORE YOUR EYES BY
HOUDINI

AFTER SEEING HIS EXHIBI-
TION THIS WEEK YOU CAN
HAVE A THOUSAND THRILLS
AT HOME. BE YOUR OWN
MEDIUM. IT IS POSITIVELY
EASY AND SIMPLE.
OPEN FORUM OF FIVE MINUTES AFTER ACT.
MR. HOUDINI CANNOT GIVE A PRIVATE AUDIENCE
WITHOUT APPOINTMENT

Margery said spirits made ectoplasm pour from her nose, mouth and ears. The goo looked like bread dough.

Final curtain?

"I want my show to be the best of its kind whilst I am alive. When I am dead there will not be another like it."
— Harry

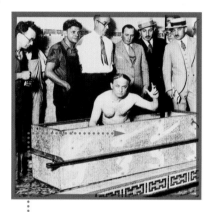

Harry tried to use his survival in the airless coffin to help others. He said people in collapsed mines might live longer if they stayed calm and breathed slowly.

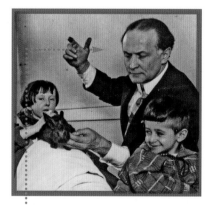

Harry was loved by many for his kindness to children. But he had enemies — did an angry medium hire the student who punched him?

At Christmastime in 1925, Harry opened a show called "HOUDINI" at a Broadway theater in New York. No longer a vaudeville act, it competed with the best theater shows and actors. He was very proud to have gained such fame and respectability.

What a show! It opened with magic tricks and illusions, including one like the Dismembering Trick Harry had seen Dr. Lynn perform long ago (see page 6). "HOUDINI" featured Harry's most famous escapes, including the Water-Torture Cell, and finished with him debunking spiritualism.

Harry could never ignore a challenge. When another magician in New York began to get good reviews for his Buried Alive Escape, Harry claimed that he could stay in an airtight casket longer. The other magician lasted without air for an hour, so Harry knew what he had to do — he immediately began three weeks of strenuous training.

On August 5, 1926, Harry climbed into a coffin that held only three or four minutes' worth of air. The coffin was lowered into a swimming pool. An hour and a half later, Harry emerged. He was confused and hallucinating, but he had beaten the other magician.

Harry went on tour in the fall of 1926, bringing along a bronze casket for publicity. In Montreal, Quebec, he entertained some university students in his dressing room. One student asked, "Is it true, Mr. Houdini, that you can resist the hardest blows struck to the abdomen?" Before Harry could prepare himself, the student began punching him in the stomach. After a few hits, the fellow stopped, but the damage was done.

Harry made it through the next show and headed for Detroit, Michigan, by train. But his pain was too severe. A doctor was summoned to meet him at the train station. It turned out that Harry already had appendicitis (swelling of the appendix) and the punches had made it worse.

Despite his suffering, Harry was determined to perform that night. He collapsed during the show but finished it, then had to be rushed to hospital to have his appendix removed. But it was too late. His appendix had ruptured and spread infection through his body.

Harry died on October 31, 1926. His body was taken back to New York and buried in the same coffin he'd brought along on his tour. But Harry Houdini's fame lives on. He was able to tap into people's desire to be amazed by things they couldn't understand. Through determination, hard work and incredible talent, Harry changed the world of magic forever.

HOUDINI DEAD

HARDEEN
Inherits his Brother's Secrets

"FOURTH: I give, devise and bequeath to my brother, THEODORE, Professionally known as "HARDEEN," all my theatrical effects, new mysteries and illusions and accompanying paraphernalia, to be burnt and destroyed upon his death."

Houdini

HOUDINI'S WILL
Makes possible the continuance of HOUDINI'S MASTER MYSTERIES

Houdini's brother Hardeen went on performing many of Harry's tricks and escapes after Harry's death.

One reason Harry became so famous was because, for 16 years after his death, Bess hired a publicist to keep his legend alive.

Bess, seen here with Hardeen at Harry's grave, held séances every October 31. She hoped Harry would speak from the grave. After ten years, Bess gave up. But other people are still trying to contact Harry.

At first newspapers wrote that Houdini's secrets died with him. But he actually passed on his props and techniques to his brother Hardeen.

November 1, 1926
LONG BEACH PRESS-TELEGRAM
HOUDINI KEEPS HIS SECRETS
*** Tricks Go to Grave With Magician

DETROIT, Nov. 1. – (By Associated Press.) – Harry Houdini's mysterious feats of escape, which thrilled spectators throughout the world in his life, today were locked in the mystery of death. The magician, hailed by his fellow workers as the greatest of them all, died here last night, taking with him the secrets of how he escaped from manacles, chains, coffins, straight jackets and other contrivances, performances which no other man ever had duplicated under his challenge.

Although Houdini wrote ... on magic, the fruit ... century experi... manag...

"His stunts were his own, and not adapted from some thing some one else h... done," said B. M. L. Er... Vice President of the So... of American Magician... explanation... eri...

Harry's life at a glance

1874 March 24 — Ehrich Weisz is born in Budapest, Hungary

1876 Ehrich's father, Mayer Samuel Weisz, leaves for the United States to find a job

Wilhelmina Beatrice ("Bess") Rahner, Ehrich's future wife, is born

1878 September — Ehrich's mother, Cecilia Steiner Weisz, and children join Rabbi Weisz in Appleton, Wisconsin, where he has a small congregation. The family's name is changed to Weiss.

1883 Ehrich performs acrobatics at a backyard circus in Milwaukee, Wisconsin, and calls himself "Ehrich, the Prince of the Air"

1886 Ehrich runs away from home for a year

1887 Rabbi Weiss moves to New York City. Ehrich, and then the rest of the family, join him. Ehrich, now known as Ehrie, gets a job at a necktie cutting company.

1891 Ehrie teams up with his friend Jacob Hyman in a magic act called "The Brothers Houdini." Ehrie starts calling himself Harry Houdini.

1892 October 5 — Harry's father dies after surgery for cancer

1893 The Brothers Houdini perform at the World's Fair in Chicago, Illinois. Their tricks include Needle Swallowing.

1894 Jacob Hyman leaves the Brothers Houdini and is replaced for a short time by Harry's brother Theodore

June 22 — Harry marries performer Bess Rahner, after knowing her for only three weeks. Bess replaces Theo in the stage act, now known as "The Houdinis."

1895 The Houdinis become known for their trick, Metamorphosis. Harry also begins performing handcuff escapes.

1896 On tour in New Brunswick, in Canada, Harry tries on a straitjacket and gets the idea of trying to escape from it

1898 With no money, Harry and Bess are forced to live with his mother in New York. Harry thinks about leaving the magic business and offers to sell the secrets behind his tricks. No one buys them.

1899 Martin Beck, a theater manager, sees Harry's handcuff act in St. Paul, Minnesota, and hires him. Within months, Harry is performing at top vaudeville houses across the United States.

1900 Harry and Bess sail to Europe. He spends most of the next five years there, performing and becoming a star.

1904 Harry performs his legendary Mirror Cuff handcuff escape in London, England

Harry buys a house in New York, which becomes his home for the rest of his life

1905 Harry and Bess return to live in the United States

1907 January — Harry makes his first Manacled Bridge Jump in Rochester, New York

1908 January 27 — Harry begins performing the Milk Can Escape in St. Louis, Missouri

April 10 — Harry escapes after being tied up with tire chains, car tires and locks from the Weed Tire Chain Grip Company

Harry publishes *The Unmasking of Robert-Houdin*

1910 March 18 — Harry wins a prize for making the first airplane flight in Australia, staying in the air for three and a half minutes

1911 Harry is injured when strapped into a bag while performing in Detroit, Michigan. He's forced to rest for two weeks.

1912 July 7 — Harry performs his Underwater Box Escape in New York Harbor. He repeats the feat nightly in a huge tank in a theater in the city.

September 21 — Harry first performs the Water-Torture Cell Escape in Berlin

1913 Harry legally changes his name to Harry Houdini

July 16 — Harry's mother dies

1914 May — Harry sails home from Europe on board a ship with former US President Theodore Roosevelt

August — World War I begins

In New York, Harry presents the trick Walking Through a Brick Wall

1915 Harry introduces the Suspended Straitjacket Escape

1916 Harry begins organizing the Film Development Corporation to process film

1917 The United States enters World War I. Harry volunteers for the army but is turned down because of his age.

1918 During his show in New York, Harry makes an elephant disappear. He also teaches soldiers how to escape from handcuffs.

World War I ends

1919 Harry's first movie, *The Master Mystery*, opens. It is successful worldwide.

Harry stars in the movie *The Grim Game*

1920 The 1920 edition of Funk & Wagnall's dictionary includes the verb "houdinize"

Harry stars in the movie *Terror Island*

Harry becomes friends with the famous author Sir Arthur Conan Doyle

1921 Harry forms the Houdini Picture Corporation, his own movie production company

Harry stars in the movie *The Soul of Bronze*

Harry publishes his book *Miracle Mongers and Their Methods*, about people who eat fire, swallow poison and more

1922 The movie *The Man from Beyond* opens, written by, produced by and starring Harry

1923 Harry's sixth and last movie, *Haldane of the Secret Service*, opens

1924 Harry tours the United States lecturing against fraudulent mediums

Harry publishes *The Unmasking — A Magician Among the Spirits*

Harry joins the *Scientific American* magazine committee to investigate fake mediums

July — Harry has his first sittings with Mina Crandon, also known as Margery, a well-known medium from Boston, Massachusetts

1925 Harry begins his show "HOUDINI"

1926 Harry testifies before a Congress committee investigating fake mediums

August 5 — Harry survives in a sealed coffin, underwater, for an hour and a half

October 31 — Harry dies in Detroit of a ruptured appendix

Nobody had a life like mine!

Visit Harry

American Museum of Magic,
Marshall, Michigan

At this museum you can see a milk can from Harry's famous Milk Can Escape, as well as posters, books, magazines and equipment used by performers in magic shows around the world. (Call ahead to make an appointment.)

Houdini Historical Center,
Appleton, Wisconsin

Located in the Outagamie Museum, this center celebrates one of the most famous people to live in Appleton. Get a map and take a walking tour of places that were important in Harry's early years.

Houdini Museum,
Scranton, Pennsylvania

Harry performed in Scranton often on his vaudeville tours. You can enjoy a magic show at this museum, watch clips from Harry's movie *The Master Mystery*, and see locks, straitjackets and more. (Call for opening hours.)

Harry and Bess's townhouse,
278 West 113th Street,
New York, New York

You can't go into the house Harry lived in for so many years, but some people feel that Harry still haunts his home. Harry, of course, didn't believe in ghosts.

You can see plenty of photos of Bess and me at the Library of Congress Web site!

Index